# Girl give yourself a Break

A 52-week Guided
Self-Care Journal for the
Boss Woman, Busy Mom and Caregiver

Annisha Gabriel

Copyright © 2020 Annisha Gabriel
Written by Annisha Gabriel

All rights reserved, including the right to reproduce this book or portions thereof in any form whatsoever without permission of the author

This Journal Belongs to :

## Why I created this book?

As a female entrepreneur, I can totally identify with the fact that we tend to put everyone and everything before ourselves. We are always in turbo mode and often try to figure out why we feel the way we do, overwhelmed; fatigued; irritable and the list goes on. There are times I have looked myself in the mirror and don't even recognize the person staring back. We all need a sanity break at some point or we will crash and burn, leaving our family, friends and business behind.

I made an investment in myself by working with a life coach, and this has changed my life significantly. She helped me to understand the importance of slowing down ever so often and putting myself first, by doing things that brought me joy. I had to blow the dust off some things I had pushed aside due to my constant hustle. It is amazing how much of a difference it makes when you schedule time for yourself even though it is only once per week for starters.

I looked around my circle of female friends and realized I was not the only one constantly on the go and neglecting herself while everyone and everything is taken care of. So we made a commitment to ourselves to schedule "me time" into our weekly schedules and by doing so, we have seen a significant difference in the way we show up for our businesses and others.

# How to use this book

The beginning of the journal contains various categories of ideas to assist you with each week's activity.

Each week you are asked some guided questions that helps open your awareness of your emotions for the present day and the week ahead. This is very important because a lot of times we tend to push our emotions aside, when we just need to acknowledge and deal with them.

A category for the weeks' activity is suggested for the first 26 weeks and you can either choose an activity from the list provided or find your own within that category. For the last 26 weeks, you will choose your categories and activities. Plan ahead and reserve some time on your schedule for some "me-time" each week. The activities should last a minimum of 30 minutes, so it does not take up too much of your already busy schedule.

It is always good to reflect on our goals, sometimes we miss them and other times we hit them. This helps us to identify what is working and where improvements are needed. Note pages are included so you can put your thoughts and feeling on paper and get them out of head. Writing has been said to be therapeutic and can also help release stress and anxiety.

# Self Care Prompts and Categories

## Eating:
- Make yourself a healthy meal (not buy)
- Make yourself a smoothie
- Cook something you have been meaning to try
- Slowly sip on your favorite hot beverage
- Increase your water intake

(infuse fruit in it if you do not like drinking water)
- Bake something just because
- Eat your favorite frozen treat
- Treat yourself to a special dinner

## Recharge/ Relax:
- Meditate/Pray/ Be still for 15-20 at least
- Do some breathing exercises/Focus on your breathing for about 5 minutes
- Go to bed early/ Get enough sleep
- Unplug from technology
- Binge watch your favorite show
- Watch a chick flick
- Read a book you have been meaning to read
- Listen to a podcast or audiobook

## Get Creative:
- Draw
- Paint something on Canvas
- Paint a stone
- Try a DIY craft project that
- interests you
- Try gardening, dig your hand in the dirt or purchase 1 plant and care for it
- Knitting
- Crochet
- Sewing

# Self Care Prompts and Categories

## **Get Moving:**

- Go for a walk (as exercise)
- Take a leisurely walk at a park or around the neighborhood
- Dance like no one is looking – put on your favorite up beat song and bust a move
- Sing at the top of your lungs, like
- no one is listening
- Go on a hike
- Do an intense workout

## **Writing:**

- Start journaling - how do you feel about the upcoming week and why?
- Write 5 things you are grateful/thankful for
- Write a letter to your younger
- self (what is the one thing you would love to tell her? /what advise can you give her?)
- Write yourself an appreciation letter
- Write yourself a love note
- Make a list of 5 things you are
- really good at but don't get the time to do and schedule 2 of them over the weeks to come
- Make a list of the persons who
- genuinely got your back and you trust, then schedule time to catch up with them
- Make a list of things you want to do in life
- Make a list of 5 things that brings a smile to your face
- Write 10 positive affirmations to repeat to yourself often and post then where you see them daily
- Do a brain dump – write out whatever is on your mind no matter how it sounds – just get it out

# Self Care Prompts and Categories

### Go out:
- Spend time with friends
- Go see a movie at your favorite theatre, all by yourself
- Go shopping
- Spend recreational time with your family/friends/pet

### Pamper Yourself:
- Put on a face mask
- Mani and Pedicure
- Get a massage
- Take a long bath/ shower (candles,
- scented oils, music, the works)
- Try aromatherapy, use an oil
- diffuser or burner to fill the air

### Caring for your Emotions:
- Ask for help when you need it- Call
- a friend you trust to disclose how you are feeling and talk things out
- Be compassionate to yourself –
- Embrace your feeling, cry if you need to
- Do something you love often
- Create an Emotional Survival Kit (things that lift your mood)
    - list of your favorite songs (Create more than one Playlists)
    - list of movies you like to watch over and over again
    - motivational quotes/YouTube Videos
- Look yourself in the mirror as if looking at a friend, what would you say to her/him right now?
- Revisit old photos of happy moments

# Let the journey begin

## Week One

Date _____

How are you feeling today?

_____

How are you feeling about the upcoming week?

☐ Ready ☐ Organized ☐ Calm ☐ Stressed ☐ Overwhelmed

## Activity Category

**Writing**

*Start Journaling*

_____

How do you feel about what you chose?
☐ I got this! ☐ Not sure ☐ A bit Anxious

Which day will you choose to make time for yourself this week?
☐ Mon. ☐ Tues. ☐ Wed. ☐ Thurs. ☐ Fri. ☐ Sat. ☐ Sun.

## Week in Review

Did you show yourself some love this past week?
☐ Yes! ☐ Didn't get the time to

How did you feel after completing this week's activity?
If you were unable to complete it, how do you feel about that?
☐ Really good ☐ I can do better ☐ Not good

Would you do this activity again?
☐ Most definitely ☐ Maybe ☐ Nah, not for me

# How are you feeling about the upcoming week? —Why?

## Note to Self

## Week Two

Date _____

### How are you feeling today?

_____

### How are you feeling about the upcoming week?

☐ Ready ☐ Organized ☐ Calm ☐ Stressed ☐ Overwhelmed

## Activity Category

**Pamper Yourself**

_____

How do you feel about what you chose?
☐ I got this! ☐ Not sure ☐ A bit Anxious

Which day will you choose to make time for yourself this week?
☐ Mon. ☐ Tues. ☐ Wed. ☐ Thurs. ☐ Fri. ☐ Sat. ☐ Sun.

## Week in Review

Did you show yourself some love this past week?
☐ Yes! ☐ Didn't get the time to

How did you feel after completing this week's activity?
If you were unable to complete it, how do you feel about that?
☐ Really good ☐ I can do better ☐ Not good

Would you do this activity again?
☐ Most definitely ☐ Maybe ☐ Nah, not for me

## How are you feeling about the upcoming week? — Why?

## Note to Self

# Week Three

**Date** _____

### How are you feeling today?
_____

### How are you feeling about the upcoming week?

☐ Ready ☐ Organized ☐ Calm ☐ Stressed ☐ Overwhelmed

## Activity Category
**Recharge and Relax**

_____

How do you feel about what you chose?
☐ I got this! ☐ Not sure ☐ A bit Anxious

Which day will you choose to make time for yourself this week?
☐ Mon. ☐ Tues. ☐ Wed. ☐ Thurs. ☐ Fri. ☐ Sat. ☐ Sun.

## Week in Review

Did you show yourself some love this past week?
☐ Yes! ☐ Didn't get the time to

How did you feel after completing this week's activity?
If you were unable to complete it, how do you feel about that?
☐ Really good ☐ I can do better ☐ Not good

Would you do this activity again?
☐ Most definitely ☐ Maybe ☐ Nah, not for me

## How are you feeling about the upcoming week? —Why?

## Note to Self

## Week Four

Date _____

How are you feeling today?

_____

How are you feeling about the upcoming week?

☐ Ready ☐ Organized ☐ Calm ☐ Stressed ☐ Overwhelmed

## Activity Category

**Get Moving**

_____

How do you feel about what you chose?
☐ I got this! ☐ Not sure ☐ A bit Anxious

Which day will you choose to make time for yourself this week?
☐ Mon. ☐ Tues. ☐ Wed. ☐ Thurs. ☐ Fri. ☐ Sat. ☐ Sun.

## Week in Review

Did you show yourself some love this past week?
☐ Yes! ☐ Didn't get the time to

How did you feel after completing this week's activity?
If you were unable to complete it, how do you feel about that?
☐ Really good ☐ I can do better ☐ Not good

Would you do this activity again?
☐ Most definitely ☐ Maybe ☐ Nah, not for me

## How are you feeling about the upcoming week? Why?

### Note to Self

# Introspection

Which activity did you enjoy most this past month?

_____
_____

Why did you enjoy this one the most?

_____
_____
_____
_____

Were you able to commit to taking time out for you each week?

☐ Yes  ☐ No

How do you feel about that?

_____
_____
_____
_____
_____
_____
_____

# Your Space

## Week Five

Date _____

How are you feeling today?

_____

How are you feeling about the upcoming week?

☐ Ready ☐ Organized ☐ Calm ☐ Stressed ☐ Overwhelmed

## Activity Category
**Go Out/ Socialize**

_____

How do you feel about what you chose?
☐ I got this! ☐ Not sure ☐ A bit Anxious

Which day will you choose to make time for yourself this week?
☐ Mon. ☐ Tues. ☐ Wed. ☐ Thurs. ☐ Fri. ☐ Sat. ☐ Sun.

## Week in Review

Did you show yourself some love this past week?
☐ Yes! ☐ Didn't get the time to

How did you feel after completing this week's activity?
If you were unable to complete it, how do you feel about that?
☐ Really good ☐ I can do better ☐ Not good

Would you do this activity again?
☐ Most definitely ☐ Maybe ☐ Nah, not for me

## How are you feeling about the upcoming week? Why?

### Note to Self

## Week Six

Date _____

### How are you feeling today?
_____

### How are you feeling about the upcoming week?

☐ Ready ☐ Organized ☐ Calm ☐ Stressed ☐ Overwhelmed

## Activity Category
**Writing**

_____

How do you feel about what you chose?
☐ I got this! ☐ Not sure ☐ A bit Anxious

Which day will you choose to make time for yourself this week?
☐ Mon. ☐ Tues. ☐ Wed. ☐ Thurs. ☐ Fri. ☐ Sat. ☐ Sun.

## Week in Review

Did you show yourself some love this past week?
☐ Yes! ☐ Didn't get the time to

How did you feel after completing this week's activity?
If you were unable to complete it, how do you feel about that?
☐ Really good ☐ I can do better ☐ Not good

Would you do this activity again?
☐ Most definitely ☐ Maybe ☐ Nah, not for me

## How are you feeling about the upcoming week? — Why?

## Note to Self

## Week Seven

Date _____

### How are you feeling today?

_____

### How are you feeling about the upcoming week?

☐ Ready ☐ Organized ☐ Calm ☐ Stressed ☐ Overwhelmed

## Activity Category

**Get Creative**

_____

How do you feel about what you chose?
☐ I got this! ☐ Not sure ☐ A bit Anxious

Which day will you choose to make time for yourself this week?
☐ Mon. ☐ Tues. ☐ Wed. ☐ Thurs. ☐ Fri. ☐ Sat. ☐ Sun.

## Week in Review

Did you show yourself some love this past week?
☐ Yes! ☐ Didn't get the time to

How did you feel after completing this week's activity?
If you were unable to complete it, how do you feel about that?
☐ Really good ☐ I can do better ☐ Not good

Would you do this activity again?
☐ Most definitely ☐ Maybe ☐ Nah, not for me

## How are you feeling about the upcoming week? —Why?

### Note to Self

## Week Eight

Date _____

How are you feeling today?

_____

How are you feeling about the upcoming week?

☐ Ready ☐ Organized ☐ Calm ☐ Stressed ☐ Overwhelmed

## Activity Category

**Caring for your Emotions**

_____

How do you feel about what you chose?
☐ I got this! ☐ Not sure ☐ A bit Anxious

Which day will you choose to make time for yourself this week?
☐ Mon. ☐ Tues. ☐ Wed. ☐ Thurs. ☐ Fri. ☐ Sat. ☐ Sun.

## Week in Review

Did you show yourself some love this past week?
☐ Yes! ☐ Didn't get the time to

How did you feel after completing this week's activity?
If you were unable to complete it, how do you feel about that?
☐ Really good ☐ I can do better ☐ Not good

Would you do this activity again?
☐ Most definitely ☐ Maybe ☐ Nah, not for me

## How are you feeling about the upcoming week? Why?

### Note to Self

# Introspection

### Which activity did you enjoy most this past month?

___

### Why did you enjoy this one the most?

___

### Were you able to commit to taking time out for you each week?

☐ Yes   ☐ No

### How do you feel about that?

___

# Your Space

## Week Nine

Date _____

### How are you feeling today?

_____

### How are you feeling about the upcoming week?

☐ Ready ☐ Organized ☐ Calm ☐ Stressed ☐ Overwhelmed

## Activity Category

**Eating**

_____

How do you feel about what you chose?
☐ I got this! ☐ Not sure ☐ A bit Anxious

Which day will you choose to make time for yourself this week?
☐ Mon. ☐ Tues. ☐ Wed. ☐ Thurs. ☐ Fri. ☐ Sat. ☐ Sun.

## Week in Review

Did you show yourself some love this past week?
☐ Yes! ☐ Didn't get the time to

How did you feel after completing this week's activity?
If you were unable to complete it, how do you feel about that?
☐ Really good ☐ I can do better ☐ Not good

Would you do this activity again?
☐ Most definitely ☐ Maybe ☐ Nah, not for me

## How are you feeling about the upcoming week? — Why?

### Note to Self

## Week Ten

Date _____

How are you feeling today?

_____

How are you feeling about the upcoming week?

☐ Ready ☐ Organized ☐ Calm ☐ Stressed ☐ Overwhelmed

## Activity Category
**Pamper Yourself**

_____

How do you feel about what you chose?
☐ I got this! ☐ Not sure ☐ A bit Anxious

Which day will you choose to make time for yourself this week?
☐ Mon. ☐ Tues. ☐ Wed. ☐ Thurs. ☐ Fri. ☐ Sat. ☐ Sun.

## Week in Review

Did you show yourself some love this past week?
☐ Yes! ☐ Didn't get the time to

How did you feel after completing this week's activity?
If you were unable to complete it, how do you feel about that?
☐ Really good ☐ I can do better ☐ Not good

Would you do this activity again?
☐ Most definitely ☐ Maybe ☐ Nah, not for me

## How are you feeling about the upcoming week? — Why?

### Note to Self

## Week Eleven

Date _____

How are you feeling today?

_____

How are you feeling about the upcoming week?

☐ Ready ☐ Organized ☐ Calm ☐ Stressed ☐ Overwhelmed

## Activity Category

**Get Moving**

_____

How do you feel about what you chose?
☐ I got this! ☐ Not sure ☐ A bit Anxious

Which day will you choose to make time for yourself this week?
☐ Mon. ☐ Tues. ☐ Wed. ☐ Thurs. ☐ Fri. ☐ Sat. ☐ Sun.

## Week in Review

Did you show yourself some love this past week?
☐ Yes! ☐ Didn't get the time to

How did you feel after completing this week's activity?
If you were unable to complete it, how do you feel about that?
☐ Really good ☐ I can do better ☐ Not good

Would you do this activity again?
☐ Most definitely ☐ Maybe ☐ Nah, not for me

## How are you feeling about the upcoming week? Why?

### Note to Self

## Week Twelve

Date _____

How are you feeling today?
_____

How are you feeling about the upcoming week?

☐ Ready ☐ Organized ☐ Calm ☐ Stressed ☐ Overwhelmed

## Activity Category
**Writing**

_____

How do you feel about what you chose?
☐ I got this! ☐ Not sure ☐ A bit Anxious

Which day will you choose to make time for yourself this week?
☐ Mon. ☐ Tues. ☐ Wed. ☐ Thurs. ☐ Fri. ☐ Sat. ☐ Sun.

## Week in Review

Did you show yourself some love this past week?
☐ Yes! ☐ Didn't get the time to

How did you feel after completing this week's activity?
If you were unable to complete it, how do you feel about that?
☐ Really good ☐ I can do better ☐ Not good

Would you do this activity again?
☐ Most definitely ☐ Maybe ☐ Nah, not for me

## How are you feeling about the upcoming week? Why?

### Note to Self

# Introspection

Which activity did you enjoy most this past month?

_____
_____

Why did you enjoy this one the most?

_____
_____
_____

Were you able to commit to taking time out for you each week?

☐ Yes   ☐ No

How do you feel about that?

_____
_____
_____
_____
_____

# Your Space

## Week Thirteen

How are you feeling today?

_____

How are you feeling about the upcoming week?

☐ Ready ☐ Organized ☐ Calm ☐ Stressed ☐ Overwhelmed

## Activity Category
**Relax and Recharge**

_____

How do you feel about what you chose?
☐ I got this! ☐ Not sure ☐ A bit Anxious

Which day will you choose to make time for yourself this week?
☐ Mon. ☐ Tues. ☐ Wed. ☐ Thurs. ☐ Fri. ☐ Sat. ☐ Sun.

## Week in Review

Did you show yourself some love this past week?
☐ Yes! ☐ Didn't get the time to

How did you feel after completing this week's activity?
If you were unable to complete it, how do you feel about that?
☐ Really good ☐ I can do better ☐ Not good

Would you do this activity again?
☐ Most definitely ☐ Maybe ☐ Nah, not for me

## How are you feeling about the upcoming week? — Why?

## Note to Self

## Week Fourteen

Date _____

### How are you feeling today?
_____

### How are you feeling about the upcoming week?

☐ Ready ☐ Organized ☐ Calm ☐ Stressed ☐ Overwhelmed

## Activity Category
**Get Creative**

_____

How do you feel about what you chose?
☐ I got this! ☐ Not sure ☐ A bit Anxious

Which day will you choose to make time for yourself this week?
☐ Mon. ☐ Tues. ☐ Wed. ☐ Thurs. ☐ Fri. ☐ Sat. ☐ Sun.

## Week in Review

Did you show yourself some love this past week?
☐ Yes! ☐ Didn't get the time to

How did you feel after completing this week's activity?
If you were unable to complete it, how do you feel about that?
☐ Really good ☐ I can do better ☐ Not good

Would you do this activity again?
☐ Most definitely ☐ Maybe ☐ Nah, not for me

## How are you feeling about the upcoming week? — Why?

### Note to Self

## Week Fifteen

Date _____

### How are you feeling today?
_____

### How are you feeling about the upcoming week?

☐ Ready ☐ Organized ☐ Calm ☐ Stressed ☐ Overwhelmed

## Activity Category
**Go Out/ Socialize**

_____

How do you feel about what you chose?
☐ I got this! ☐ Not sure ☐ A bit Anxious

Which day will you choose to make time for yourself this week?
☐ Mon. ☐ Tues. ☐ Wed. ☐ Thurs. ☐ Fri. ☐ Sat. ☐ Sun.

## Week in Review

Did you show yourself some love this past week?
☐ Yes! ☐ Didn't get the time to

How did you feel after completing this week's activity?
If you were unable to complete it, how do you feel about that?
☐ Really good ☐ I can do better ☐ Not good

Would you do this activity again?
☐ Most definitely ☐ Maybe ☐ Nah, not for me

# How are you feeling about the upcoming week? —Why?

## Note to Self

## Week Sixteen

Date _____

How are you feeling today?

_____

How are you feeling about the upcoming week?

☐ Ready ☐ Organized ☐ Calm ☐ Stressed ☐ Overwhelmed

## Activity Category

**Caring for your Emotions**

_____

How do you feel about what you chose?
☐ I got this! ☐ Not sure ☐ A bit Anxious

Which day will you choose to make time for yourself this week?
☐ Mon. ☐ Tues. ☐ Wed. ☐ Thurs. ☐ Fri. ☐ Sat. ☐ Sun.

## Week in Review

Did you show yourself some love this past week?
☐ Yes! ☐ Didn't get the time to

How did you feel after completing this week's activity?
If you were unable to complete it, how do you feel about that?
☐ Really good ☐ I can do better ☐ Not good

Would you do this activity again?
☐ Most definitely ☐ Maybe ☐ Nah, not for me

## How are you feeling about the upcoming week? Why?

### Note to Self

# Introspection

Which activity did you enjoy most this past month?

Why did you enjoy this one the most?

Were you able to commit to taking time out for you each week?

☐ Yes   ☐ No

How do you feel about that?

# Your Space

## Week Seventeen

Date _____

### How are you feeling today?
_____

### How are you feeling about the upcoming week?

☐ Ready ☐ Organized ☐ Calm ☐ Stressed ☐ Overwhelmed

## Activity Category

**Eating**

_____

How do you feel about what you chose?
☐ I got this! ☐ Not sure ☐ A bit Anxious

Which day will you choose to make time for yourself this week?
☐ Mon. ☐ Tues. ☐ Wed. ☐ Thurs. ☐ Fri. ☐ Sat. ☐ Sun.

## Week in Review

Did you show yourself some love this past week?
☐ Yes! ☐ Didn't get the time to

How did you feel after completing this week's activity?
If you were unable to complete it, how do you feel about that?
☐ Really good ☐ I can do better ☐ Not good

Would you do this activity again?
☐ Most definitely ☐ Maybe ☐ Nah, not for me

## How are you feeling about the upcoming week? Why?

### Note to Self

## Week Eighteen

Date _____

How are you feeling today?

_____

How are you feeling about the upcoming week?

☐ Ready ☐ Organized ☐ Calm ☐ Stressed ☐ Overwhelmed

## Activity Category

**Writing**

_____

How do you feel about what you chose?
☐ I got this! ☐ Not sure ☐ A bit Anxious

Which day will you choose to make time for yourself this week?
☐ Mon. ☐ Tues. ☐ Wed. ☐ Thurs. ☐ Fri. ☐ Sat. ☐ Sun.

## Week in Review

Did you show yourself some love this past week?
☐ Yes! ☐ Didn't get the time to

How did you feel after completing this week's activity?
If you were unable to complete it, how do you feel about that?
☐ Really good ☐ I can do better ☐ Not good

Would you do this activity again?
☐ Most definitely ☐ Maybe ☐ Nah, not for me

## How are you feeling about the upcoming week? Why?

## Note to Self

## Week Nineteen

Date _____

How are you feeling today?

_____

How are you feeling about the upcoming week?

☐ Ready ☐ Organized ☐ Calm ☐ Stressed ☐ Overwhelmed

## Activity Category

**Pamper Yourself**

_____

How do you feel about what you chose?
☐ I got this! ☐ Not sure ☐ A bit Anxious

Which day will you choose to make time for yourself this week?
☐ Mon. ☐ Tues. ☐ Wed. ☐ Thurs. ☐ Fri. ☐ Sat. ☐ Sun.

## Week in Review

Did you show yourself some love this past week?
☐ Yes! ☐ Didn't get the time to

How did you feel after completing this week's activity?
If you were unable to complete it, how do you feel about that?
☐ Really good ☐ I can do better ☐ Not good

Would you do this activity again?
☐ Most definitely ☐ Maybe ☐ Nah, not for me

## How are you feeling about the upcoming week? —Why?

### Note to Self

## Week Twenty

Date _____

How are you feeling today?

_____

How are you feeling about the upcoming week?

☐ Ready ☐ Organized ☐ Calm ☐ Stressed ☐ Overwhelmed

## Activity Category

**Get Creative**

_____

How do you feel about what you chose?
☐ I got this! ☐ Not sure ☐ A bit Anxious

Which day will you choose to make time for yourself this week?
☐ Mon. ☐ Tues. ☐ Wed. ☐ Thurs. ☐ Fri. ☐ Sat. ☐ Sun.

## Week in Review

Did you show yourself some love this past week?
☐ Yes! ☐ Didn't get the time to

How did you feel after completing this week's activity?
If you were unable to complete it, how do you feel about that?
☐ Really good ☐ I can do better ☐ Not good

Would you do this activity again?
☐ Most definitely ☐ Maybe ☐ Nah, not for me

## How are you feeling about the upcoming week? — Why?

## Note to Self

# Introspection

**Which activity did you enjoy most this past month?**

_____
_____

**Why did you enjoy this one the most?**

_____
_____
_____

**Were you able to commit to taking time out for you each week?**

☐ Yes    ☐ No

**How do you feel about that?**

_____
_____
_____
_____
_____

# Your Space

## Week Twenty-One

Date _____

### How are you feeling today?

_____

### How are you feeling about the upcoming week?

☐ Ready ☐ Organized ☐ Calm ☐ Stressed ☐ Overwhelmed

## Activity Category

**Get Moving**

_____

How do you feel about what you chose?
☐ I got this! ☐ Not sure ☐ A bit Anxious

Which day will you choose to make time for yourself this week?
☐ Mon. ☐ Tues. ☐ Wed. ☐ Thurs. ☐ Fri. ☐ Sat. ☐ Sun.

## Week in Review

Did you show yourself some love this past week?
☐ Yes! ☐ Didn't get the time to

How did you feel after completing this week's activity?
If you were unable to complete it, how do you feel about that?
☐ Really good ☐ I can do better ☐ Not good

Would you do this activity again?
☐ Most definitely ☐ Maybe ☐ Nah, not for me

## How are you feeling about the upcoming week? — Why?

### Note to Self

## Week Twenty-Two

Date _____

### How are you feeling today?
_____

### How are you feeling about the upcoming week?

☐ Ready ☐ Organized ☐ Calm ☐ Stressed ☐ Overwhelmed

## Activity Category

**Caring for your Emotions**

_____

How do you feel about what you chose?
☐ I got this! ☐ Not sure ☐ A bit Anxious

Which day will you choose to make time for yourself this week?
☐ Mon. ☐ Tues. ☐ Wed. ☐ Thurs. ☐ Fri. ☐ Sat. ☐ Sun.

## Week in Review

Did you show yourself some love this past week?
☐ Yes! ☐ Didn't get the time to

How did you feel after completing this week's activity?
If you were unable to complete it, how do you feel about that?
☐ Really good ☐ I can do better ☐ Not good

Would you do this activity again?
☐ Most definitely ☐ Maybe ☐ Nah, not for me

## How are you feeling about the upcoming week? Why?

### Note to Self

### Week Twenty-Three

Date _____

How are you feeling today?

_____

How are you feeling about the upcoming week?

☐ Ready ☐ Organized ☐ Calm ☐ Stressed ☐ Overwhelmed

---

### Activity Category

**Relax and Recharge**

_____

How do you feel about what you chose?
☐ I got this! ☐ Not sure ☐ A bit Anxious

Which day will you choose to make time for yourself this week?
☐ Mon. ☐ Tues. ☐ Wed. ☐ Thurs. ☐ Fri. ☐ Sat. ☐ Sun.

---

### Week in Review

Did you show yourself some love this past week?
☐ Yes! ☐ Didn't get the time to

How did you feel after completing this week's activity?
If you were unable to complete it, how do you feel about that?
☐ Really good ☐ I can do better ☐ Not good

Would you do this activity again?
☐ Most definitely ☐ Maybe ☐ Nah, not for me

# How are you feeling about the upcoming week? —Why?

## Note to Self

## Week Twenty-Four

Date _____

### How are you feeling today?

_____

### How are you feeling about the upcoming week?

☐ Ready ☐ Organized ☐ Calm ☐ Stressed ☐ Overwhelmed

## Activity Category

**Writing**

_____

How do you feel about what you chose?
☐ I got this! ☐ Not sure ☐ A bit Anxious

Which day will you choose to make time for yourself this week?
☐ Mon. ☐ Tues. ☐ Wed. ☐ Thurs. ☐ Fri. ☐ Sat. ☐ Sun.

## Week in Review

Did you show yourself some love this past week?
☐ Yes! ☐ Didn't get the time to

How did you feel after completing this week's activity?
If you were unable to complete it, how do you feel about that?
☐ Really good ☐ I can do better ☐ Not good

Would you do this activity again?
☐ Most definitely ☐ Maybe ☐ Nah, not for me

## How are you feeling about the upcoming week? — Why?

## Note to Self

# Introspection

### Which activity did you enjoy most this past month?

_____
_____

### Why did you enjoy this one the most?

_____
_____
_____
_____

### Were you able to commit to taking time out for you each week?

☐ Yes     ☐ No

### How do you feel about that?

_____
_____
_____
_____
_____
_____

# Your Space

## Week Twenty-Five

Date _____

How are you feeling today?

_____

How are you feeling about the upcoming week?

☐ Ready ☐ Organized ☐ Calm ☐ Stressed ☐ Overwhelmed

### Activity Category

**Eating**

_____

How do you feel about what you chose?
☐ I got this! ☐ Not sure ☐ A bit Anxious

Which day will you choose to make time for yourself this week?
☐ Mon. ☐ Tues. ☐ Wed. ☐ Thurs. ☐ Fri. ☐ Sat. ☐ Sun.

### Week in Review

Did you show yourself some love this past week?
☐ Yes! ☐ Didn't get the time to

How did you feel after completing this week's activity?
If you were unable to complete it, how do you feel about that?
☐ Really good ☐ I can do better ☐ Not good

Would you do this activity again?
☐ Most definitely ☐ Maybe ☐ Nah, not for me

## How are you feeling about the upcoming week? — Why?

### Note to Self

# Week Twenty-Six

Date _____

## How are you feeling today?
_____

## How are you feeling about the upcoming week?

☐ Ready ☐ Organized ☐ Calm ☐ Stressed ☐ Overwhelmed

## Activity Category
**Pamper Yourself**

_____

How do you feel about what you chose?
☐ I got this! ☐ Not sure ☐ A bit Anxious

Which day will you choose to make time for yourself this week?
☐ Mon. ☐ Tues. ☐ Wed. ☐ Thurs. ☐ Fri. ☐ Sat. ☐ Sun.

## Week in Review

Did you show yourself some love this past week?
☐ Yes! ☐ Didn't get the time to

How did you feel after completing this week's activity?
If you were unable to complete it, how do you feel about that?
☐ Really good ☐ I can do better ☐ Not good

Would you do this activity again?
☐ Most definitely ☐ Maybe ☐ Nah, not for me

# How are you feeling about the upcoming week? — Why?

## Note to Self

## Week Twenty-Seven

Date _____

### How are you feeling today?
_____

### How are you feeling about the upcoming week?

☐ Ready ☐ Organized ☐ Calm ☐ Stressed ☐ Overwhelmed

## Activity Category

_____

### How do you feel about what you chose?
☐ I got this! ☐ Not sure ☐ A bit Anxious

### Which day will you choose to make time for yourself this week?
☐ Mon. ☐ Tues. ☐ Wed. ☐ Thurs. ☐ Fri. ☐ Sat. ☐ Sun.

## Week in Review

### Did you show yourself some love this past week?
☐ Yes! ☐ Didn't get the time to

### How did you feel after completing this week's activity?
### If you were unable to complete it, how do you feel about that?
☐ Really good ☐ I can do better ☐ Not good

### Would you do this activity again?
☐ Most definitely ☐ Maybe ☐ Nah, not for me

## How are you feeling about the upcoming week? Why?

## Note to Self

## Week Twenty-Eight

Date ————

How are you feeling today?

_____

How are you feeling about the upcoming week?

☐ Ready ☐ Organized ☐ Calm ☐ Stressed ☐ Overwhelmed

## Activity Category

_____

How do you feel about what you chose?
☐ I got this! ☐ Not sure ☐ A bit Anxious

Which day will you choose to make time for yourself this week?
☐ Mon. ☐ Tues. ☐ Wed. ☐ Thurs. ☐ Fri. ☐ Sat. ☐ Sun.

## Week in Review

Did you show yourself some love this past week?
☐ Yes! ☐ Didn't get the time to

How did you feel after completing this week's activity?
If you were unable to complete it, how do you feel about that?
☐ Really good ☐ I can do better ☐ Not good

Would you do this activity again?
☐ Most definitely ☐ Maybe ☐ Nah, not for me

## How are you feeling about the upcoming week? —Why?

### Note to Self

# Introspection

Which activity did you enjoy most this past month?

_____
_____

Why did you enjoy this one the most?

_____
_____
_____
_____

Were you able to commit to taking time out for you each week?

☐ Yes   ☐ No

How do you feel about that?

_____
_____
_____
_____
_____
_____
_____

# Your Space

you are halfway there!

# Be Proud of yourself

## Week Twenty-Nine

Date _____

How are you feeling today?

_____

How are you feeling about the upcoming week?

☐ Ready ☐ Organized ☐ Calm ☐ Stressed ☐ Overwhelmed

## Activity Category

_____

How do you feel about what you chose?
☐ I got this! ☐ Not sure ☐ A bit Anxious

Which day will you choose to make time for yourself this week?
☐ Mon. ☐ Tues. ☐ Wed. ☐ Thurs. ☐ Fri. ☐ Sat. ☐ Sun.

## Week in Review

Did you show yourself some love this past week?
☐ Yes! ☐ Didn't get the time to

How did you feel after completing this week's activity?
If you were unable to complete it, how do you feel about that?
☐ Really good ☐ I can do better ☐ Not good

Would you do this activity again?
☐ Most definitely ☐ Maybe ☐ Nah, not for me

## How are you feeling about the upcoming week? — Why?

## Note to Self

## Week Thirty

Date _____

### How are you feeling today?

_____

### How are you feeling about the upcoming week?

☐ Ready ☐ Organized ☐ Calm ☐ Stressed ☐ Overwhelmed

## Activity Category

_____

### How do you feel about what you chose?
☐ I got this! ☐ Not sure ☐ A bit Anxious

### Which day will you choose to make time for yourself this week?
☐ Mon. ☐ Tues. ☐ Wed. ☐ Thurs. ☐ Fri. ☐ Sat. ☐ Sun.

## Week in Review

### Did you show yourself some love this past week?
☐ Yes! ☐ Didn't get the time to

### How did you feel after completing this week's activity?
If you were unable to complete it, how do you feel about that?
☐ Really good ☐ I can do better ☐ Not good

### Would you do this activity again?
☐ Most definitely ☐ Maybe ☐ Nah, not for me

## How are you feeling about the upcoming week? Why?

## Note to Self

## Week Thirty-One

Date _____

How are you feeling today?

_____

How are you feeling about the upcoming week?

☐ Ready ☐ Organized ☐ Calm ☐ Stressed ☐ Overwhelmed

## Activity Category

_____

How do you feel about what you chose?
☐ I got this! ☐ Not sure ☐ A bit Anxious

Which day will you choose to make time for yourself this week?
☐ Mon. ☐ Tues. ☐ Wed. ☐ Thurs. ☐ Fri. ☐ Sat. ☐ Sun.

## Week in Review

Did you show yourself some love this past week?
☐ Yes! ☐ Didn't get the time to

How did you feel after completing this week's activity?
If you were unable to complete it, how do you feel about that?
☐ Really good ☐ I can do better ☐ Not good

Would you do this activity again?
☐ Most definitely ☐ Maybe ☐ Nah, not for me

## How are you feeling about the upcoming week? Why?

## Note to Self

## Week Thirty-Two

Date _____

How are you feeling today?

_____

How are you feeling about the upcoming week?

☐ Ready ☐ Organized ☐ Calm ☐ Stressed ☐ Overwhelmed

## Activity Category

_____

How do you feel about what you chose?
☐ I got this! ☐ Not sure ☐ A bit Anxious

Which day will you choose to make time for yourself this week?
☐ Mon. ☐ Tues. ☐ Wed. ☐ Thurs. ☐ Fri. ☐ Sat. ☐ Sun.

## Week in Review

Did you show yourself some love this past week?
☐ Yes! ☐ Didn't get the time to

How did you feel after completing this week's activity?
If you were unable to complete it, how do you feel about that?
☐ Really good ☐ I can do better ☐ Not good

Would you do this activity again?
☐ Most definitely ☐ Maybe ☐ Nah, not for me

## How are you feeling about the upcoming week? Why?

## Note to Self

# Introspection

**Which activity did you enjoy most this past month?**

_____
_____

**Why did you enjoy this one the most?**

_____
_____
_____
_____

**Were you able to commit to taking time out for you each week?**

☐ Yes   ☐ No

**How do you feel about that?**

_____
_____
_____
_____
_____
_____
_____

# Your Space

## Week Thirty-Three

Date _____

How are you feeling today?

_____

How are you feeling about the upcoming week?

☐ Ready ☐ Organized ☐ Calm ☐ Stressed ☐ Overwhelmed

## Activity Category

_____

How do you feel about what you chose?
☐ I got this! ☐ Not sure ☐ A bit Anxious

Which day will you choose to make time for yourself this week?
☐ Mon. ☐ Tues. ☐ Wed. ☐ Thurs. ☐ Fri. ☐ Sat. ☐ Sun.

## Week in Review

Did you show yourself some love this past week?
☐ Yes! ☐ Didn't get the time to

How did you feel after completing this week's activity?
If you were unable to complete it, how do you feel about that?
☐ Really good ☐ I can do better ☐ Not good

Would you do this activity again?
☐ Most definitely ☐ Maybe ☐ Nah, not for me

## How are you feeling about the upcoming week? — Why?

### Note to Self

## Week Thirty-Four

Date _____

How are you feeling today?

_____

How are you feeling about the upcoming week?

☐ Ready ☐ Organized ☐ Calm ☐ Stressed ☐ Overwhelmed

## Activity Category

_____

How do you feel about what you chose?
☐ I got this! ☐ Not sure ☐ A bit Anxious

Which day will you choose to make time for yourself this week?
☐ Mon. ☐ Tues. ☐ Wed. ☐ Thurs. ☐ Fri. ☐ Sat. ☐ Sun.

## Week in Review

Did you show yourself some love this past week?
☐ Yes! ☐ Didn't get the time to

How did you feel after completing this week's activity?
If you were unable to complete it, how do you feel about that?
☐ Really good ☐ I can do better ☐ Not good

Would you do this activity again?
☐ Most definitely ☐ Maybe ☐ Nah, not for me

## How are you feeling about the upcoming week? Why?

## Note to Self

## Week Thirty-Five

Date _____

How are you feeling today?

_____

How are you feeling about the upcoming week?

☐ Ready ☐ Organized ☐ Calm ☐ Stressed ☐ Overwhelmed

## Activity Category

_____

How do you feel about what you chose?
☐ I got this! ☐ Not sure ☐ A bit Anxious

Which day will you choose to make time for yourself this week?
☐ Mon. ☐ Tues. ☐ Wed. ☐ Thurs. ☐ Fri. ☐ Sat. ☐ Sun.

## Week in Review

Did you show yourself some love this past week?
☐ Yes! ☐ Didn't get the time to

How did you feel after completing this week's activity?
If you were unable to complete it, how do you feel about that?
☐ Really good ☐ I can do better ☐ Not good

Would you do this activity again?
☐ Most definitely ☐ Maybe ☐ Nah, not for me

## How are you feeling about the upcoming week? — Why?

## Note to Self

## Week Thirty-Six

Date _____

How are you feeling today?

_____

How are you feeling about the upcoming week?

☐ Ready ☐ Organized ☐ Calm ☐ Stressed ☐ Overwhelmed

## Activity Category

_____

How do you feel about what you chose?
☐ I got this! ☐ Not sure ☐ A bit Anxious

Which day will you choose to make time for yourself this week?
☐ Mon. ☐ Tues. ☐ Wed. ☐ Thurs. ☐ Fri. ☐ Sat. ☐ Sun.

## Week in Review

Did you show yourself some love this past week?
☐ Yes! ☐ Didn't get the time to

How did you feel after completing this week's activity?
If you were unable to complete it, how do you feel about that?
☐ Really good ☐ I can do better ☐ Not good

Would you do this activity again?
☐ Most definitely ☐ Maybe ☐ Nah, not for me

## How are you feeling about the upcoming week? —Why?

### Note to Self

# Introspection

### Which activity did you enjoy most this past month?

_____
_____

### Why did you enjoy this one the most?

_____
_____
_____
_____

### Were you able to commit to taking time out for you each week?

☐ Yes   ☐ No

### How do you feel about that?

_____
_____
_____
_____
_____
_____

# Your Space

## Week Thirty-Seven

Date _____

How are you feeling today?

_____

How are you feeling about the upcoming week?

☐ Ready ☐ Organized ☐ Calm ☐ Stressed ☐ Overwhelmed

## Activity Category

_____

How do you feel about what you chose?
☐ I got this! ☐ Not sure ☐ A bit Anxious

Which day will you choose to make time for yourself this week?
☐ Mon. ☐ Tues. ☐ Wed. ☐ Thurs. ☐ Fri. ☐ Sat. ☐ Sun.

## Week in Review

Did you show yourself some love this past week?
☐ Yes! ☐ Didn't get the time to

How did you feel after completing this week's activity?
If you were unable to complete it, how do you feel about that?
☐ Really good ☐ I can do better ☐ Not good

Would you do this activity again?
☐ Most definitely ☐ Maybe ☐ Nah, not for me

## How are you feeling about the upcoming week? Why?

### Note to Self

## Week Thirty-Eight

Date _____

How are you feeling today?

_____

How are you feeling about the upcoming week?

☐ Ready ☐ Organized ☐ Calm ☐ Stressed ☐ Overwhelmed

## Activity Category

_____

How do you feel about what you chose?
☐ I got this! ☐ Not sure ☐ A bit Anxious

Which day will you choose to make time for yourself this week?
☐ Mon. ☐ Tues. ☐ Wed. ☐ Thurs. ☐ Fri. ☐ Sat. ☐ Sun.

## Week in Review

Did you show yourself some love this past week?
☐ Yes! ☐ Didn't get the time to

How did you feel after completing this week's activity?
If you were unable to complete it, how do you feel about that?
☐ Really good ☐ I can do better ☐ Not good

Would you do this activity again?
☐ Most definitely ☐ Maybe ☐ Nah, not for me

## How are you feeling about the upcoming week? — Why?

## Note to Self

## Week Thirty-Nine

Date _____

How are you feeling today?

_____

How are you feeling about the upcoming week?

☐ Ready ☐ Organized ☐ Calm ☐ Stressed ☐ Overwhelmed

## Activity Category

_____

How do you feel about what you chose?
☐ I got this! ☐ Not sure ☐ A bit Anxious

Which day will you choose to make time for yourself this week?
☐ Mon. ☐ Tues. ☐ Wed. ☐ Thurs. ☐ Fri. ☐ Sat. ☐ Sun.

## Week in Review

Did you show yourself some love this past week?
☐ Yes! ☐ Didn't get the time to

How did you feel after completing this week's activity?
If you were unable to complete it, how do you feel about that?
☐ Really good ☐ I can do better ☐ Not good

Would you do this activity again?
☐ Most definitely ☐ Maybe ☐ Nah, not for me

## How are you feeling about the upcoming week? — Why?

### Note to Self

## Week Forty

Date _____

How are you feeling today?

_____

How are you feeling about the upcoming week?

☐ Ready ☐ Organized ☐ Calm ☐ Stressed ☐ Overwhelmed

## Activity Category

_____

How do you feel about what you chose?
☐ I got this! ☐ Not sure ☐ A bit Anxious

Which day will you choose to make time for yourself this week?
☐ Mon. ☐ Tues. ☐ Wed. ☐ Thurs. ☐ Fri. ☐ Sat. ☐ Sun.

## Week in Review

Did you show yourself some love this past week?
☐ Yes! ☐ Didn't get the time to

How did you feel after completing this week's activity?
If you were unable to complete it, how do you feel about that?
☐ Really good ☐ I can do better ☐ Not good

Would you do this activity again?
☐ Most definitely ☐ Maybe ☐ Nah, not for me

## How are you feeling about the upcoming week? Why?

## Note to Self

# Introspection

Which activity did you enjoy most this past month?

Why did you enjoy this one the most?

Were you able to commit to taking time out for you each week?

☐ Yes  ☐ No

How do you feel about that?

# Your Space

## Week Forty-One

Date _____

How are you feeling today?

_____

How are you feeling about the upcoming week?

☐ Ready ☐ Organized ☐ Calm ☐ Stressed ☐ Overwhelmed

## Activity Category

_____

How do you feel about what you chose?
☐ I got this! ☐ Not sure ☐ A bit Anxious

Which day will you choose to make time for yourself this week?
☐ Mon. ☐ Tues. ☐ Wed. ☐ Thurs. ☐ Fri. ☐ Sat. ☐ Sun.

## Week in Review

Did you show yourself some love this past week?
☐ Yes! ☐ Didn't get the time to

How did you feel after completing this week's activity?
If you were unable to complete it, how do you feel about that?
☐ Really good ☐ I can do better ☐ Not good

Would you do this activity again?
☐ Most definitely ☐ Maybe ☐ Nah, not for me

## How are you feeling about the upcoming week? Why?

## Note to Self

## Week Forty-Two

Date _____

### How are you feeling today?

_____

### How are you feeling about the upcoming week?

☐ Ready ☐ Organized ☐ Calm ☐ Stressed ☐ Overwhelmed

## Activity Category

_____

How do you feel about what you chose?
☐ I got this! ☐ Not sure ☐ A bit Anxious

Which day will you choose to make time for yourself this week?
☐ Mon. ☐ Tues. ☐ Wed. ☐ Thurs. ☐ Fri. ☐ Sat. ☐ Sun.

## Week in Review

Did you show yourself some love this past week?
☐ Yes! ☐ Didn't get the time to

How did you feel after completing this week's activity?
If you were unable to complete it, how do you feel about that?
☐ Really good ☐ I can do better ☐ Not good

Would you do this activity again?
☐ Most definitely ☐ Maybe ☐ Nah, not for me

## How are you feeling about the upcoming week? Why?

### Note to Self

## Week Forty-Three

Date _____

How are you feeling today?

_____

How are you feeling about the upcoming week?

☐ Ready ☐ Organized ☐ Calm ☐ Stressed ☐ Overwhelmed

## Activity Category

_____

How do you feel about what you chose?
☐ I got this! ☐ Not sure ☐ A bit Anxious

Which day will you choose to make time for yourself this week?
☐ Mon. ☐ Tues. ☐ Wed. ☐ Thurs. ☐ Fri. ☐ Sat. ☐ Sun.

## Week in Review

Did you show yourself some love this past week?
☐ Yes! ☐ Didn't get the time to

How did you feel after completing this week's activity?
If you were unable to complete it, how do you feel about that?
☐ Really good ☐ I can do better ☐ Not good

Would you do this activity again?
☐ Most definitely ☐ Maybe ☐ Nah, not for me

## How are you feeling about the upcoming week? —Why?

### Note to Self

# Week Forty-Four

Date _____

How are you feeling today?

_____

How are you feeling about the upcoming week?

☐ Ready ☐ Organized ☐ Calm ☐ Stressed ☐ Overwhelmed

## Activity Category

_____

How do you feel about what you chose?
☐ I got this! ☐ Not sure ☐ A bit Anxious

Which day will you choose to make time for yourself this week?
☐ Mon. ☐ Tues. ☐ Wed. ☐ Thurs. ☐ Fri. ☐ Sat. ☐ Sun.

## Week in Review

Did you show yourself some love this past week?
☐ Yes! ☐ Didn't get the time to

How did you feel after completing this week's activity?
If you were unable to complete it, how do you feel about that?
☐ Really good ☐ I can do better ☐ Not good

Would you do this activity again?
☐ Most definitely ☐ Maybe ☐ Nah, not for me

## How are you feeling about the upcoming week? — Why?

### Note to Self

# Introspection

Which activity did you enjoy most this past month?

_____
_____

Why did you enjoy this one the most?

_____
_____
_____
_____

Were you able to commit to taking time out for you each week?

☐ Yes  ☐ No

How do you feel about that?

_____
_____
_____
_____
_____
_____

# Your Space

## Week Forty-Five

Date _____

How are you feeling today?

_____

How are you feeling about the upcoming week?

☐ Ready ☐ Organized ☐ Calm ☐ Stressed ☐ Overwhelmed

## Activity Category

_____

How do you feel about what you chose?
☐ I got this! ☐ Not sure ☐ A bit Anxious

Which day will you choose to make time for yourself this week?
☐ Mon. ☐ Tues. ☐ Wed. ☐ Thurs. ☐ Fri. ☐ Sat. ☐ Sun.

## Week in Review

Did you show yourself some love this past week?
☐ Yes! ☐ Didn't get the time to

How did you feel after completing this week's activity?
If you were unable to complete it, how do you feel about that?
☐ Really good ☐ I can do better ☐ Not good

Would you do this activity again?
☐ Most definitely ☐ Maybe ☐ Nah, not for me

## How are you feeling about the upcoming week? — Why?

## Note to Self

## Week Forty-Six

Date _____

How are you feeling today?

_____

How are you feeling about the upcoming week?

☐ Ready ☐ Organized ☐ Calm ☐ Stressed ☐ Overwhelmed

## Activity Category

_____

How do you feel about what you chose?
☐ I got this! ☐ Not sure ☐ A bit Anxious

Which day will you choose to make time for yourself this week?
☐ Mon. ☐ Tues. ☐ Wed. ☐ Thurs. ☐ Fri. ☐ Sat. ☐ Sun.

## Week in Review

Did you show yourself some love this past week?
☐ Yes! ☐ Didn't get the time to

How did you feel after completing this week's activity?
If you were unable to complete it, how do you feel about that?
☐ Really good ☐ I can do better ☐ Not good

Would you do this activity again?
☐ Most definitely ☐ Maybe ☐ Nah, not for me

## How are you feeling about the upcoming week? — Why?

## Note to Self

## Week Forty-Seven

Date _____

How are you feeling today?

_____

How are you feeling about the upcoming week?

☐ Ready ☐ Organized ☐ Calm ☐ Stressed ☐ Overwhelmed

## Activity Category

_____

How do you feel about what you chose?
☐ I got this! ☐ Not sure ☐ A bit Anxious

Which day will you choose to make time for yourself this week?
☐ Mon. ☐ Tues. ☐ Wed. ☐ Thurs. ☐ Fri. ☐ Sat. ☐ Sun.

## Week in Review

Did you show yourself some love this past week?
☐ Yes! ☐ Didn't get the time to

How did you feel after completing this week's activity?
If you were unable to complete it, how do you feel about that?
☐ Really good ☐ I can do better ☐ Not good

Would you do this activity again?
☐ Most definitely ☐ Maybe ☐ Nah, not for me

# How are you feeling about the upcoming week? Why?

## Note to Self

## Week Forty Eight

Date _____

How are you feeling today?

_____

How are you feeling about the upcoming week?

☐ Ready ☐ Organized ☐ Calm ☐ Stressed ☐ Overwhelmed

## Activity Category

_____

How do you feel about what you chose?
☐ I got this! ☐ Not sure ☐ A bit Anxious

Which day will you choose to make time for yourself this week?
☐ Mon. ☐ Tues. ☐ Wed. ☐ Thurs. ☐ Fri. ☐ Sat. ☐ Sun.

## Week in Review

Did you show yourself some love this past week?
☐ Yes! ☐ Didn't get the time to

How did you feel after completing this week's activity?
If you were unable to complete it, how do you feel about that?
☐ Really good ☐ I can do better ☐ Not good

Would you do this activity again?
☐ Most definitely ☐ Maybe ☐ Nah, not for me

## How are you feeling about the upcoming week? — Why?

## Note to Self

# Introspection

Which activity did you enjoy most this past month?

_____
_____

Why did you enjoy this one the most?

_____
_____
_____
_____

Were you able to commit to taking time out for you each week?

☐ Yes  ☐ No

How do you feel about that?

_____
_____
_____
_____
_____
_____
_____

# Your Space

## Week Forty-Nine

Date _____

How are you feeling today?

_____

How are you feeling about the upcoming week?

☐ Ready ☐ Organized ☐ Calm ☐ Stressed ☐ Overwhelmed

## Activity Category

_____

How do you feel about what you chose?
☐ I got this! ☐ Not sure ☐ A bit Anxious

Which day will you choose to make time for yourself this week?
☐ Mon. ☐ Tues. ☐ Wed. ☐ Thurs. ☐ Fri. ☐ Sat. ☐ Sun.

## Week in Review

Did you show yourself some love this past week?
☐ Yes! ☐ Didn't get the time to

How did you feel after completing this week's activity?
If you were unable to complete it, how do you feel about that?
☐ Really good ☐ I can do better ☐ Not good

Would you do this activity again?
☐ Most definitely ☐ Maybe ☐ Nah, not for me

## How are you feeling about the upcoming week? Why?

### Note to Self

## Week Fifty

Date _____

How are you feeling today?

_____

How are you feeling about the upcoming week?

☐ Ready ☐ Organized ☐ Calm ☐ Stressed ☐ Overwhelmed

## Activity Category

_____

How do you feel about what you chose?
☐ I got this! ☐ Not sure ☐ A bit Anxious

Which day will you choose to make time for yourself this week?
☐ Mon. ☐ Tues. ☐ Wed. ☐ Thurs. ☐ Fri. ☐ Sat. ☐ Sun.

## Week in Review

Did you show yourself some love this past week?
☐ Yes! ☐ Didn't get the time to

How did you feel after completing this week's activity?
If you were unable to complete it, how do you feel about that?
☐ Really good ☐ I can do better ☐ Not good

Would you do this activity again?
☐ Most definitely ☐ Maybe ☐ Nah, not for me

## How are you feeling about the upcoming week? Why?

### Note to Self

## Week Fifty-One

Date _____

How are you feeling today?

_____

How are you feeling about the upcoming week?

☐ Ready ☐ Organized ☐ Calm ☐ Stressed ☐ Overwhelmed

## Activity Category

_____

How do you feel about what you chose?
☐ I got this! ☐ Not sure ☐ A bit Anxious

Which day will you choose to make time for yourself this week?
☐ Mon. ☐ Tues. ☐ Wed. ☐ Thurs. ☐ Fri. ☐ Sat. ☐ Sun.

## Week in Review

Did you show yourself some love this past week?
☐ Yes! ☐ Didn't get the time to

How did you feel after completing this week's activity?
If you were unable to complete it, how do you feel about that?
☐ Really good ☐ I can do better ☐ Not good

Would you do this activity again?
☐ Most definitely ☐ Maybe ☐ Nah, not for me

## How are you feeling about the upcoming week? Why?

## Note to Self

## Week Fifty-Two

Date _____

### How are you feeling today?

_____

### How are you feeling about the upcoming week?

☐ Ready ☐ Organized ☐ Calm ☐ Stressed ☐ Overwhelmed

## Activity Category

_____

How do you feel about what you chose?
☐ I got this! ☐ Not sure ☐ A bit Anxious

Which day will you choose to make time for yourself this week?
☐ Mon. ☐ Tues. ☐ Wed. ☐ Thurs. ☐ Fri. ☐ Sat. ☐ Sun.

## Week in Review

Did you show yourself some love this past week?
☐ Yes! ☐ Didn't get the time to

How did you feel after completing this week's activity?
If you were unable to complete it, how do you feel about that?
☐ Really good ☐ I can do better ☐ Not good

Would you do this activity again?
☐ Most definitely ☐ Maybe ☐ Nah, not for me

## How are you feeling about the upcoming week? Why?

### Note to Self

# Introspection

Which activity did you enjoy most this past month?

_____
_____

Why did you enjoy this one the most?

_____
_____
_____
_____

Were you able to commit to taking time out for you each week?

☐ Yes  ☐ No

How do you feel about that?

_____
_____
_____
_____
_____
_____

# Introspection

# Congratulations

You have done it. Your activity now is to Celebrate!

Made in the USA
Middletown, DE
29 November 2020